ren —
love how joyous &
blooming your spirit
is. I love that you la
Youtube, DIY, &, just
around on urban ou...
So happy — that you jus
here & that I got to know y
your light & passion. This book
lucky to have you. I hope ..
gives you as much care & comfort at
you bring into the world.
All my love &
gratitude always.
❤)S—

JUNE 2021

Birthday Girl
by Sheila J Sadr

Not a Cult
Los Angeles, CA

ISBN: 978-1-945649-40-0

Edited by Safia Elhillo
Proofread by Rhiannon McGavin
Cover design by Faye Orlove and Cassidy Trier
Editorial design by Julianna Sy

Not a Cult
Los Angeles, CA

To those who didn't survive.

Contents

bionic woman

full moon   cloaked shadow
who are you without all these
    other hands? what are
you made of when
    you go untouched?
    wet moth   fluttering pussy
        all metallic silk, hot and electric
honey   you natural
    mechanical thing
built of so many parts,   interlink
    coconut oiled
        nuts and bolts, a stew
a limited mess   No
    warranty, just a pair of latex
gloves and speculum to test your
    open wounds. hot breath
pitted apple   outside skin
take the seeds that grew you
    and what do you have?
        cyanide
    are you still a living thing if
all your insides beg
    for death?

I

Soghatee

We congregate at the dining table.
The rice and stew, a welcome mat
against our tongues. Mommon   speaks us jamaat
and I utter,   a gathering. Our words
break bread   together. We make a meal
of aush reshteh and nammak, and they become
blood and sugar   in our mouths. Farsi is the first
souvenir we receive as children. Turns into glass we
now ferry   with our teeth. How long   can we make
this heirloom   last? Translation,   the mint collecting
at the bridge of our plates.   Leaving   us full,
leaving us   hungry.

Confessional

I find my seat in the church choir
of my sister's laugh.
Her smile, holy
water on Sundays.
Her teeth outstretched, the only religion
I wish to claim my name.
Bless'd be her laugh, how it
rings into the air,
brings sunshine
on a dim day. Bless
the days she sounds
of church
bell and hallelujahs,
of prayers and stained
glass. How I
sit in all this glory,
light it like
a candle, hold it
like a god.

Ode to My Heart

A time capsule Baba Bozorg
buried in October dirt. His gift
earthed in pomegranate.
Mommon's—half-bitten peach.
Resown in this pink orchard.
This bookshelf. A wind-
chime ballad. Mine—the homemaker.
Breadwinner. The meat packer,
dirty-worker. Mine. The hymn,
the mosque's stubborn meditation.
My family's first prayer answered.
Bless'd be my heart.
This sensitive crate. .
All pump and fever.
Bless'd be the hands who made this.
The winter moons who shaped
this clay to spring. The apple bloom
in Mommon's belly.
The first rose
Baba smelled between her hair.
Bless'd be this late-blossomed first love.
The first tale God spoke
in Baba Bozorg's ear, whispered
into his veins, into kismet
symphony. A promise. A name
with every press firm against his chest.
Bless'd be his own stuttered globe.
How he offered his spare beats to me.
Bless'd be his story threading
into mine. This golden silk
we fold together. The only place
I will ever serve him tea.
This heart—this homecoming.

The giver
and his lullaby of push
and blood.

Kharjee

What am I to make of the question mark and blank

spaces that   I am? Where hijab   does not call

to Iran but to Muslim?   And *merci* is a language

traded between two rebellious cities?   What am I

to make   of the blank space where only I lie standing?

The television screen does not bear Iranian

against her belly.   The models and poets and teachers do the same.

Where is the world pregnant with me

but in Iran?

Where my American

does not belong. Where my American

is a divorced father.

What is the Iran?

What does it look like?   My mother,

pulling me in like an ocean yet still

threatening to drown me?

What is an Iran in an American?

Does it exist?

Does it

breathe?

Does it stand
and live on its own?

Has it ever survived?

Home Key

I want to love someone
with my father's eyes.
Someone who looks like a cool
bed after a long drunk night.
Floats along my skin like a northwest
breeze waiting for the winter. I want
to love someone who smells like clean laundry
and a home-cooked meal after nine p.m.
A love that always turns the light off
when I fall asleep. Wipes as much makeup as they can
off my face. Moves the laptop from my side.
Pulls the sheets in. Calls me home
with their hips. Their lips, the lock and key.
Their hands, the radiator/AC. Calls me
home and I become the child,
racing in before sunset.

History Lesson

A song excavates the smell
of Ameh Maryam's kitchen on Eid
from a decade ago, lets the rice
lift in its drum beat and the mahi to fry over
Googoosh's vibrato. Baba says
he listens to Persian music
so he doesn't get depressed.
And now I know the price of a plane ticket.
How many years he had
to turn the knob on the radio
to hear a foreign country
hold his hostage. Now I know how many times
he could not hold his mommon's hand or
drink in the sunlight that bore him in a metro desert.
And I know now
an education costs in america—a wanderer
in a country that refuses to enunciate
my father's name, curses my dinner,
holds contempt
like a bag of shaken wasps.

Origin Story

In this house, all we do is clean. Wipe countertops, sweep
   the floor. Rinse our teacups, hang them
to dry. In this house, the party ends when sleep gnaws us
to the marrow. But the chai is always hot, always
boiling. Leftovers still packed in tin—the second and third
refrigerator tucked away in the garage. In this house
after all the guests leave, we pace around the kitchen.   Float
around our mother like driftwood. In this house,   Mommon
always starts the fire, crisps the esfand   in her heat.
Lights the smoke to let out the   superstition.

Learning to Pray
After Kaveh Akbar

Prayer is a lighthouse the woman never visits. Only
when drunk with the blood of another god does
she bow her head against another prayer, weeps in
the funeral pyre of her own womb. Begs god for a
better death. The woman's prayers are linen soaked
in rum and honey, are my mother's constant
scrubbing. Her bellyache against the dinner table.
Her nerves, their incessant frying. When the
woman prays, Mommon and I go looking for her
cries. Find only a confessional. The woman's
prayers are a sad occasion. A holiday that reeks with
grief. The woman's prayers are a search party for
herself. Her father, his abandonment. A godless
prayer. Her own empty nesting my mother
scavenges to fill. The only ache I can't harbor
keeping. Truth is I've never heard my sister pray,
but I know it's the only thing she does. In her silent
ask, her pleading back and forth, her bending teeth
against all its padded walls.

And So My Mother was a Child Once

and my father was too,
and they played house before
the house was built. Kissed hands
of khalehs and amoos before they left
for bed. Smelled the tea unspooling in estekans.
My mother was a child before her grape skin
peeled back for another man. Painted fruit
in oils and Chicago burn. Her honeycomb eyes
sticky for something more.
A room I will never know.
Did my mother dream like me?
A far-off land and a place all her own.
Did she pray for it at 23, two babies
on her arm? Her hair, a sonnet of almond flour.
My father, only a boy, running
against the alleyways. Baba joon waddling
into his baba bozorg's arms.
Sneaking water on a fasting day,
tasting the sunset sugar.

Epigraph from Anxiety on the Tarmac

birthday girl

birth   day girl

day girl night girl   side

girl failed girl broken girl

sidenote collateral damage

girl

give me everything you have

inside yourself

girl all that good honey girl

good girl

good girl

bad girl

open

mouth puckered lip girl

the *type*

I'd marry girl

the slut girl

the who could ever love you

with all this heart girl

all this baggage girl

this too much

for your own good girl

you're a good girl, right?

all

following directions

type girl   one misstep

and there is glass girl   the

you better watch out girl

call you *queen* girl but all I mean is

I am afraid

afraid of everything girl

that one step off the precipice

is the wrong step girl

the orange juice

with pulp girl

the hour late girl

                              misses

                    every
                    damn
                    appointment
                    girl

                              the smart
                              in useless ways girl

the type I'd marry

              girl

   the forever girl

          the only one I've got girl

            the one I'd stick by

                    when all my lights go out

                                        girl

      haunted girl

everything is haunting her girl

He Calls Me *Queen*

and here I am.
Crushing so many bones
to make purple wine
    Rising
from harvest to transverse
his earthy mouth.
Bless the men who drink the wine
and taste the fruit that came before.
He calls me queen,
and I liquefy to syrup.   My skin
browning a butternut squash.
The sweat, hot and alive, I wish to turn
my tongue against.   A kink
I never thought so divine.
To be kissed
for the fig you have always been,   a gift
wrapped in ambered skin. Let me
spill all over you. Lick me
clean up off the floor.
I am a wet thing anyways.
Spilling my contents with every tip.
Every turn, a mess I never
wish cleaned up. He called me queen,
and I became a season.
One who knows how the moon
turns. How she howls. One who lets everything
fall and turn to ash. One who sips
her own juice and waits against the wind.
Who cools. Turns golden. Turns honey
dark. Bundles. Breaks. Brings new life.

Love Poem
After Kristin Chang

I look up
our star signs and your eyes

christen me a holy place
Take down your hair   Kiss me

Let us make home out of the coffee shop.
Count the notches on our foreheads.

You are becoming the hymn
I find myself humming to

holding so tightly   I wish
to trace our fault lines before

we tonic on the couch
I time capsule   this joy

I am a cradled harp against your belly. I trace
my feet on the porch of love and know

love poems make sense now   the love
poems make sense now   the love poems

question how long will this last?
carry this moment   please

like an offering around my neck.
What if we made love?

Could I have your Sundays?
Your softer hours, the eyelash on your chin?

            I confess I want to know my way
around your shadow, afraid of

becoming an apparition who sits
atop your nightstand. Every time

I pray *Lord, let me keep this hour*
a little longer. I wonder if

this is a haunting or a home. A curse burning
this midday meal. Remind myself how these

keep me in your mouth
a minute longer.

Khejalat nemekeshe?

Can Mommon love me
without judgement? Anger?
Without being the ocean? The wave
pulling away right as it kisses the sand?
When did all my couplets lead back to her?

Can my sister come back to me? Bring me
summers of broken yolk in our hair when
we'd rinse away all this heat? All this
mislanguage between us now?
Can pain bring laugh lines?

I hope it does. When did my lies
fold in on themselves? Split mouth
against a diamond ring? Is falling
in love with a white boy treachery?
A lie to myself? My mother?

Has my mother become (I am) paper? Do all my
(our) words fold in on themselves again?

II

Ar-(Rahm)an

I made a man from clay and he turned me into
bone. Let me bury myself aadam under his skin.
Broke all my other faces to fit into a home he
ibrahim'ed from straw and sunlight. I followed
a boy to a pair of mountains and he left me in
the sand. Ran seven times between their aching
breasts. I ran so far I forgot my own God. My
name spilling out like oil. Turned me dirty
Zamzam against the belly of a desert. I ran so far
for a man I crumpled myself into a holy book
and he chewed me into dynamite.

Family Tree

I dreamt a snake coiled its way into a dog's head.
The tail suddenly burrowing a home into its
snout.

I waited for its breath to cut, the orchestra's final
collapse before   the lights go up.

Hamsar is used as a modifier for a partner;
means literally   of the same head.

So when they say she is sick,
(which could mean

her hands could not unknot themselves
after the stroke, or   *I hope she*

does not drive home in her condition, or
please do not anger Baba;

these pills, the last heart-
beat spares we have left in our pockets)

this means   we were a dream or
had once thought we were.

And I think of hamsar—
of the same head. The coupling

of blood. This cankered tree splintering
through our capillaries. This familial wolf that

hunts itself. The frenzied meat I hold
together. How many before me had a snake

curled against their brainstem? Gnawing its own
tail? Already finding its teeth through tissue?

How many will I rear to this table myself?
My blood is an infinite mirror. Runs thick. Runs

naked outside the house. Finds shelter
from itself. Hears the crescendo breaking.

Date Night

after Tatiana Ryckman and Paige Lewis

Do not leave me in this lamplight or a pixel
fading on a blue lit screen. Sit here

awhile. Your seat is warm and I am on the other
end in a rosy state. I boiled some water for myself. There are tea leaves

wasting their hours in a jar on the countertop. Grab them. Your mother
is not home. She could never hold us accountable here. She would ask us

to grocery store, grab ourselves by the bagful. Let us wait quiet in this electric sky.
Stay—just for a little while, as the sun tipsies its way into the skyline. Stairs below,

Mommon and Baba make morsels of the berenje and stew and I am missing
dinner, wafting only in its casual aftermath. Lately, missing you has

chewed me down to gristle. I do not see your face as a haunting
anymore, as yours has not seen mine as home, and now I am caught

missing you like the stove is on and I am locked outside. I am certain
there is a fog behind me that feels like a ghost.

So here we are: eye-to-eye more or less. Do you ever wonder why
it is only one eye? Ask me. Exchange some mouths. Holiday on

this call ten minutes longer. Tell me about your obsessions with Dragon Ball Z
and early mornings. We both know I will drag this time for much longer. Commandeer

your nine p.m. routine, a renegade to your nightly brew. Wait,   I know
           you want to go.   You're so tired—bloodshot. Don't

hang   up   the call. Greedy
                     boy. Please.   I know I am so

hungry

for our time. Why   do you like me?

Why are you here? Greedy girl.   Me, house-   fire. You,

burned everything alive—   absent   tongue. The world turns us   to rice

with every   palm,   every   rinse. A bug   writhing its way to

the surface. The water still   ashen with our dust. We don't seem to have

anymore

time. Stop!   Wait, wait. Come again?   Our signal is

dropping

out. Stay

on the line.

No, no check YOUR   connection. It's on YOUR

end. I can't   see you anymore.   Can we hang

up and try again? I'm sorry, you keep

breaking up

with me. C-can you   hear me?

How about now?

How-   how   about now?

the heart has four cavities

i watch him leave. watch him feather
into some other sky. i watch him disappear,
into alcohol maybe. into pencils/pens/
school-books, maybe. but time and the 5 south
melt us like popsicles on an august sidewalk
and i watch him come back. girlfriend in arm,
five months later. and she is blonde with
crooked teeth, and hips i bet he dreams about.
i watch them from a distance, through
the hollow glow of someone else's facebook,
or the ghost of my own instagram feed.

i watch him bring her home,
meet his family. the ones who hated me and still:
my warm colors/my mother's sharbat tongue/
my grandmother's hijab, the sumac
spilling across my brother's jawline. i watch
her get along with all his family: shoots guns without
a wince, without hesitation; eats pork
without flinching, never holding a lie
between her teeth. i watch them travel:
the grand canyon/the tropics/
to weddings i wanted to attend.

i watch them fall in love. slowly,
like a bee sting i've grown allergic to. i feel
his birthday pass like a hurricane pillaging
a nearby state. i sit in this throat-slit
silence, ease myself into the murderous water.
i watch years pass, the age and weight he gains
between his frame. i imagine how her breasts
must feel beneath the grip of his hands; i think of how
they kiss, how their lovemaking sounds.

her moans, the distant wail of butterfly wings;
and his, once belonging to me.
i've forgotten how he sounds.

i watched them graduate, among their family, and god
how i long to hate them/to cry/to stand
among them/to be his friend, hold his hand
maybe. how i long to prove i am
still worth all this time. i see her body
billowing in flip-flops and sundresses i've longed
to wear. i see her as i've always wanted to
see myself: normal/unbroken/a nurse/a wife/a mother,
i know one day i will watch
him propose. get married, see her stomach balloon
into a home: my casket, my heartbreak in utero.
a love story i have no chapter in.

Abody

My body is not a body but is a body but is   not a body but is but is not but is
a bullet I've given life to   There are some days where I don't want to be

a body or have a body or become a body   There are some days I wish I wasn't
loved for (my) body at all   That this body did not earn love or grow apple

in the tree of somebody's eye that this love grew   in an orchard
somewhere between   my hummingbird of a heart and theirs

There are some days when my body becomes ghost   When I become
the blessèd no body but then become   a nobody and (my) body becomes

the couch I am   haunted by the most   Once, a boy held
my breath in the   palm of his hand and all he felt was   flesh

the warm of breast the dark pink of areola   around his lips but
an Olympus of bodies have felt this flesh   this smile maybe

these lips and flint tongue these   hips and legs the intersection of my
arm hooked   in the crook of theirs but none have

broken through the precipice   the soggy ghost of me
the deep the dark matter that   lies beneath this skin

So my body is (becomes) just a body   a body that sinks
that turns decomp to soil   to roadway and boulevard to

kitchen sink and crushed velvet couch   to useful to some body
to my body is just a body a body ab ody abo   dy a bo dy a b od

y ab o dy a bo d y a bo d yod   y abo dy a bo dy a b ody
ab ody abo dy a   b od y bo dy ab o dy a bo d

Things They Say—This is Not a Confessional.

After Tarfia Faizullah and Vievee Francis

She has hit me several times. Calls me user. Says I'm the bully. Says I'm the _____(r).   *Asshole.* She punched me in the face once over a laptop and never apologized. They don't   believe me. He tells me I am weak. I tell him what this is: _____.   He has hit me too. I forgave him a long time ago. He told me he felt bad about it once.   They have all hit me   at some point. Both kicked me in the face and stomach when I was late. She washed the blood   from my mouth while she kept punching me against the sink. I don't like to talk about how old I was. She says I _____ them. She once   shoved a sandwich from the garbage into my mouth. She chased me around the house, broke her own   door down to do it.   I think this is a funny story now.   She punched me in the living room of a friend's house. Her diamond ring split   my lip open. We don't talk   about these things. They tell me not to. I have so many problems   now. I cling   to her legs, beg on my knees. She says   *I deserved to be   raped.* I am a magnet. After all, it's *happened so many times.*   I must be acting some way to bring it upon myself. She says I deserve   to be raped over and over until it comes out of my face. She asks me why   I didn't tell her about it before. If I loved her,   I would have said something   right away. She says I don't love her. She says this so many times I don't know what's the truth. I can't tell   what this is anymore. She says her apology was talking to me again. She says   I made her do it.   She tells me to stop mentioning it, says if I talk about it again she'll explode.   She says I will kill them both one day—give them heart attacks. My guilt   is a guillotine. They tell me to stop being so *sensitive.* He told me to   stop talking   about myself so much. He said this so many times I un-   learn my own tongue. She calls me a *bitch.* They tell me I am *selfish,   depressed.* They say I am the _____(r). They tell me I am *over-dramatic,* a *liar.* They tell me I am *lazy, rude.* She says   *There is nothing you can do;   this is just who you are.*   He called me over-dramatic once and I couldn't stop   chewing on their names.   He told me to move on. *Get over it.* They tell me *it's all in the past.* Clean   your heart. I hate   saying _abuse_, how the headache starts when I don't know   what's the truth.

A List Of Eleven People Who Broke Consent, Or Toed The Line As If They Were Inching Across Hot Coals, And Still Walk This Earth Like Wet Fish Slipping Through My Fingers Into The Sink As Mommon Teaches Me To Clean Their Iridescent Blue Scales Before Baking In The Oven At 250° For 25 Minutes.

Niloufar
Jacquline
Justin
Daniel
Jonah
Tanner
Flint
Bryce
Behdad
Randall
Kai

(There are others. I do not know their names.)

The Man Holds the Door Open

for me. Takes me out, buys me dinner.
The man folds all our laundry. Ivory and
pinks folded neatly into cupboards, black
and blues: together. The man is good.
I swear this man is good.
The man leaves my sister behind. Ignores my
brother's name. The man's face, a body
of gentle misdeeds. The man handcuffs
my friends. Bans my cousin from a hospital
bed and a routine visit. The man does not give my father
his green card. Shoves my aunt into a shoebox.
Denies her a crooked education. The man writes this
education, a history of whiteout corpses. Writes out
all the job apps. All the money made. The dollar bill. Tells us
that we should've "tried harder". The man sells me
lies, hiding themselves— a lingering ghost behind
my shoulders. The man rapes my mother.
He kills my children and sees our bodies as pastime.
Does not sit hidden or shy or looming
as he did before. No, his body heaves against
all the things I love the most, revelling
in all the mayhem. And this is personal.
All of this is so personal. But it never started
here. It never begins here really.
It began with a door and someone else
giving me permission
to walk through.

Shame

After Victoria Chang

i am afraid to be afraid   too afraid to be

              still   but still healing   still afraid to open

      all my heavy doors   that he had seen too much

              scab-picked skin   that I was afraid of him   that we

were rotten   that he was always rancid   and we were

              nothing   but bandaged apricots decaying in the august sun

      and he was afraid we had too much or not enough time

              afraid of us   afraid of me   afraid to speak but he breathed

hot lullabies into my neck   into scarlet

              corners of my pituitary   poisoned all my wearied nerves

      i used to call him *master*   used to master our loose laundry

              i refused to fold   i used to forgive

his virulent apologies after college parties   i used to be

              afraid of him   he used to be afraid of my amphibian temper

      how i waxed and waned through tempestuous waters

              afraid that he was always drowning   i am afraid of the

dark blue ghosts   their red angry heat   i am afraid to eat

    bullets of my own words   silver shrapnels

   if i eat them all   lead will seep into

     the insides of my abdomen   i'm ashamed i let

the abuse go on for so long   his light came in

    with brilliant blazing eyes and saw

   everything.

History Lesson (Reprise)

The story goes, my people were asked to hand

over oil in exchange for what they imagined

would be love.

O how they promised to hydrate.

How they gave life to another country

while pulling from their own.

And is there nothing more woman than this?

To feed those who are already full?

To deliver to arms who have already taken too much.

Relic

He was in good condition
before all these scratches, my constant
dropping. Before the time wore his paint away,
he had good polish, gold bones.
How he hunched over
a toilet bowl, shirt off. I admit,
I loved him even then.
Hand flush against his back.
Heavy breathing. He would tell me
to never move.

    I loved him sick and quiet.

I loved him loud, mouths thumb-
tacked till one of us cried. I loved him
for a while, and I can't remember why.
Or what it felt like outside the laugh
he would break into me like a thief.
I loved his lilac and heather gray. How he
toggled video games and routined clean laundry.
We would chomp on tramp house wrestling matches
and tart Long Beach music— stank faces.

    Perhaps, we loved each other

with our loneliness. Shared it like a snack,
nachos and cheese. Junk food depression.
We bit each other's cheeks till the birds
shook the night from their shoulders.
We sparked blood in each other
and neither was good or right.
I loved him for a long time,
and I can't remember what it felt like

outside of hour-and-a-half drives
to his house,

one way.

Like flat tires by razor blades. Kissing
someone else then begging him to stay,
on my knees. I remember his rage.
I think he loved me?
He could never tell me why.
But I know it was like
packaged mashed potatoes
mixed with water. I, settling
sous chef. Orange countertop
under blue lighting.

He knew how to love me sick and quiet.

I think he loved me like towels
folded hot dog style,   one way.
How he and his mother chuckled at
my thread shoved over the nervous railing.
How I crawled into bed with jeans on.
Never lifting enough weight. My constant
failings. How splintered
my porcelain is too. I only fold
horizontal now. Only wear inside clothes
inside the bed. Double-take beside the mirror.

It reminds me of him.

In the Worst Places

i am not the wanted daughter.
i am not the fix. the prize.
the happy ending.
i am the plague.
the mishap. the eye roll.
an artist by name,
disease in the flesh.
i am still my mother's
disowned child.
a gift
to return. The coat that
won't fit.
in the worst places,
i call myself the wrong address.
a mistaken turn. an accident
to the flesh I am from.
tripwire. broken ankles.
who am i to call myself love?
to give myself
a holy name.
it's not mine.
another child's.
a softer mouth
and time-kept curfew.
a girl who laughs more,
who never felt the sun
warm her skin,
the salt on her cheek.
i was mixed up long ago.
someone return me.
i am a book overdue.
i am the wrong size of myself.

Ideation

It's just a thought,

and you are afraid
of how your bones are more than bones

and how the Devil picks his teeth with you.

It's just a thought.

It is gone now.

Mommon sings to you a lullaby. But the beast
paces beneath your jaw.   Your wrists.

She whispers,

God is as close to you as your jugular

and you believed.
You have believed her for so long

your pulse forgot your name.

Called survival and death by the same tongue.

A mouth you no longer want.
How God

is the only prayer

your jugular will grip in rope burn.
Behind the closet door. It is then

in the humble silence

                                    Right?

He is as close to you as death.

III

Mommon Speaks

My daughter has dreams.

I hear them through the door.

Her voice amber fire popping, warming

my toes from the crevice.

She speaks of Indiana and poetry,

of grammar rules and grad school

and a dirty blond love 25 miles away.

She plays Red Hot Chili Peppers and dances for a future full

of my soft grandchildren.

Plans for babies and wood floorboards even though

time is now a water lily,

wilting in fog light.

I wish this future for her always.

Lungs packing and unpacking.

Tummies full of food I learned to cook from my mother

and her mother's mother.

I wish to keep her with me always.

Carpet floor. Cast iron door.

Corkboard conversation.

My daughter wishes for living rooms

and patio decks in colors I'd never pair.

In furnishings I've never seen.

But I still want her there. Right there

in the future sunlight.

Someday. Holding my hand,

learning to walk.

Mama, You Gave Birth to a Soft Girl.

You bled your way through her and she saw
cherry wine. Strawberry jam. Mama,
you gave birth to a squishy girl.
One who squirms. Who overwhelms. Who cries
at series finales and harsh words.
I know you wanted a brick girl.
With a backbone made of gold and a crown built
in steel and rhinestone.
You do not have this girl. You do not.
I mourn her stillbirth too.
Mama, you have a girl built
of redwood seedling. Of budding, fleshy plant.
Small, flimsy but very much alive. Very much outgrowing
every space. You have a girl who wilts
in the wrong color of the sky.
Who soaks in the sun cooling
a home for the ones down below.
Mama, you gave birth to a mother all your own.
You wanted a daughter who was already skyline.
But here I am, just a blueprint. Just another place waiting
to be built up. You have a soft girl, Mama. Look at her.
She is breathing. She is alive. Congratulations. She wants
your arms. Your arms. Your arms. Your arms.
Your underbrush. Your riverbed. Just as you found her
in your womb. Swimming. Soft. Growing.
For your skin is her skin.

What is Sheila Sadr?

Ask a sundial to describe
itself and it will only speak
of the shadow. Not of the star.
Cast over a slab of wood
or concrete,
our ancestors spoke
of time the way they would of
forest, or of dinner, an old friend.
Carbon and water we call her.
Years of atoms finding their way
through a mother's breaking. A father's
fall. The laugh stuck
at the bottom
of an auntie's tummy.
Grandmas in countless generations smacking
the back of a son's neck,
kissing his forehead later.
Men offering fruit in apology,
or gratitude. Two halves
of the same peach I think.
O all the songs our bodies must've danced to.
How they pickled in warmth and sweat,
in the way all our bodies have done
the same. Snaps to
the gallons of tea this bloodline has
sipped, brewed, hued. Applause
to the hands of elders turning rice:
a story with each needle thread, every spool
unspun. Applause to this tribe,
these people, how we have
survived, no matter how many
hours it may be. Hugs to this girl truly.
Twenty-three years young, you think. But look

back and count the eons
who assembled these veins, stitched
taut this skin.
How this spirit breaks
out of itself. Stretch
marks. I am here
because you are too.
And we are.
And so is the sky.
From galaxy to grain of rice.
Pile of bones
some days and sometimes only
a jar, only a ferry to
carry tears. But a home to know.
O what a home to know.

Mohr

They told me
not to call myself
a girl. To know
myself into a woman.
After all
to be a girl in this body
is to be the seeds
in every apple. To be
a woman is to crush
all those inside you
and turn them on
another man. Poison.
Sharp tack. You're
a hard bitch huh?
They tell me
that my bones are older now.
Chop one down and call me
woman with one look at the rings
on the inside. Know my worth by my
stretched-out skin.
My ass cheek. The cursive
on my legs. They check
for ghosts with flashlights
in a cooled-out room.
No girl lives in this body, they say.

> *No, this is a woman.*
> *Be proud. Be strong.*

How empowering
to burn the bones of the heart
that grew me. To forget
who built the home.

Earthed the tree. Made the flesh
of the apple you bite from.

The girl.

The seed.

The hands so young. Silly
Putty and crayon. Hazy afternoons
on a leather couch and a tv screen.
She, I say.   *She is my mother.*
Kept me alive
when I was nothing but the sky.
So to call me   *girl*   is to hold
the ground I was born from.
To pilgrim to the temple that built me.
Is to kneel. Is to
bow your head.

to the topless photos I took for an ex who asked

when I first took you, the glass illuminated
flesh tone. caramel. with two
crushed raspberries peaking
up at my eyes.

my hands had only
touched me when
he was asleep, away
on the other end and
quiet.

he warmed us up like leftovers.

in truth, I was never turned on.
he bored me over sext.
what good did it do for me now?
his cock, feeble wet cloth
wrung out in his hands. this, our
top model moment. after all, what more is
commitment than sending naked
flesh, storing it
for second helpings.

in truth, I lied.

if I ever run for office,
I hope they frame you
in the national portrait gallery, or somewhere
in the white house, maybe
where bill's pictures lie.
title it: body of lady liberty. body
in pursuit of happiness.

I am Letting Him Go Today

I am letting him go willingly. I am letting him go like a sick arm that has grown too cold. I am letting him go to a silence that only sounds like screaming. I am letting him go only to land on my grief. I let my grief go to discover a puddle of glitter. I let the glitter go   to stumble upon my voice.   I let my voice go once, only to find it climbing back up my throat. I am letting him go today to find my soulmate.   I am letting him go so my soulmate will find me and   I won't be busy.   I am letting him go like old clothing I've alway loved   but grown out of.   I am letting someone else wear him so I can stumble on to my heart again and wear her like she's back in style. I am letting my own heart speak for its damn self. I'm letting my damn self speak to find a kitchen with a home-cooked meal and the tv on, my lover saving a spot for me on the couch. I let this find me because   it is all I've ever wanted.   I am letting him go because my heart is screaming from both sides of the street. Because it is going to hurt either way so I might as well hurt alone because   at least that is going somewhere. Somewhere where I am found. Somewhere where letting go feels less like falling and more like gravity   suspending,   like floating, like   rising. I am letting him go with curled toes and gritted teeth. I am letting him go torn in two but I don't call.   I don't text back. I don't wish another way.   I call my mother instead.

I text my best friend. I find myself despite it all. I find myself in all the rubble. I rise by the hands and grip of my friends. I rise by the strength in my own back. I rise despite. I let go despite.   I survive despite it all.

On Conflation

They tell me
you are not
here anymore. That you are
gone   all I see is
your gaze hidden
in his mouth
right here

discovering tongue and teeth.
I see you behind synapses
in his eyes

How you called me tone deaf
my name laughing between
my bones. You vice grip
me no longer but you are still
in my backyard   invasive
species of overgrowth. I am still learning
to shut you out
even when all the lights go dark.

communicating is becoming
the balm of my healing so my silence is no longer
just a bandage. Though I may be
stardust spread against the windshield. I am
nowhere anymore   yet here I stand
glitter in all my glory
we tether pole

I—a winter storm   Him—a windchime
across galaxy skies but I break even
and we become a melody.

even in all my frightened parts,
our lips   now   we marvel
my hauntings in this bed   between meals   inside
all our scraps   I wish to throw parties
for all our ghosts. To blossom new
hope for an open heart   the path
of how the sun still knows to lift its head

I Watch My Ex's Ex's Story on Instagram

and somehow I'm relieved.
Funny how umbilical heartbreak can be.
I listen to her laugh, poke around with kittens,
stretch in yoga, dance against a pulsating beat
and all I feel
is my oxygen mask release in a falling plane.
A breath without restriction, without bitterness.
Kinship unearthed from a boy with roadside palms, pitstop skin.
I found home in Sisterhood
because of men who know nothing of groundskeeping.
Impatient men stuck in the teeth of patient women.
And how tenderly and generously she has picked you out.
Day by day, I breathe new air in this drowning city.
Each tap, a sticky note of hope.
Each giggle untethered, a highlight reel is born.
Each second she smiles with your name absent from her cheek,
a new holy ray of light blossoms in my chest.
In the afternoon, I carry water to a garden we nurse together.
Pot daisies in the mulch of men who know not the sweat of cultivation.
How we both smell the clean air, taste the summer wind.
For now we are free.
And men like you are archived news.
And men like you are archived news.
For now we are free.
How we both smell the clean air, taste the summer wind.
Pot daisies in the mulch of men who know not the sweat of cultivation.
In the afternoon, I carry water to a garden we nurse together.
A new holy ray of light blossoms in my chest
each second she smiles with your name absent from her cheek.
Each giggle untethered, a highlight reel is born.
Each tap, a sticky note of hope.
Day by day, I breathe new air in this drowning city
and how tenderly and generously she has picked you out.

Impatient men stuck in the teeth of patient women.
Because of men who know nothing of groundskeeping,
I found home in Sisterhood.
Kinship unearthed from a boy with roadside palms, pitstop skin.
A breath without restriction, without bitterness,
is my oxygen mask release in a falling plane.
And all I feel
stretch in yoga, dance against a pulsating beat.
I listen to her laugh, poke around with kittens.
Funny how umbilical heartbreak can be.
And somehow I'm relieved.

Joy

After Ross Gay

I know I hold onto joy
until it hurts
I know like a lover
I am scared
it will go
I know joy
is a simple view
with a demanding hiking trail
I know joy is joy
because I know it goes away
I know I hold joy
by the root
pull it by the stem
expose its sunlight in the dirt
Look at her, my joy,
with all its beginnings
and endings
I know joy is found
in every breath
I keep taking
that I choose to be alive
because I know joy exists
not in fairytales or happy endings
but in inhales and exhales
in smiles in moments
I know joy is no lifetime quilt
but the thread,

golden and unrelenting, tying
all the pieces together
Joy is my mother's cooking
My brother
falling in love
My sister putting
the wine glass down
My baba saying
I am on the right path
and although the last two
haven't happened yet
I know, I know
that day will come
because joy comes
Joy always finds a way
In the minutes
the words
the breath
the faith, the faith
is in joy
In all the silences
In the moment the muscles
in the corners of your mouth
lift or when they drop
onto a couch
relaxing
The joy of letting go
and taking in
inhale inhale
then let it go

Pussy Takes Herself Out

She gets wined and dined and seduced
on a casual Tuesday afternoon
and she is not surprised, knows her own
value by the berry count.
Pussy goes to a movie by herself.
Cries at all the sad scenes loudly. Laughs
a full belly laugh when she can.
Pussy gets a wax—
she is confused. Doesn't know why she needed this but
there she is bald and naked on the table like sashimi.
Tonight she takes herself to dinner. P.F. Chang's
most likely. Flirts with the waiter of course. She is hungry after all.
Pussy has a drink and takes her hunger to-go. Draws herself
a warm bath. She thinks, sipping on her wine,

> *to love yourself is a pleasure. An honor.*
> *What a gift you are to yourself. To have a body tethered*
> *to such a giving spirit. Gratitude. O gratitude.*

Depression is My Daughter and Now I Brush Her Hair

I know I am a mother
because I have had so many
   things escape my body.

Today my daughter sits on cold
tile. Her knees, a dry aftertaste.
I brush her hair. It
tangles. The dark coiled silk.
Tough like mine.
I brush her hair, because she asks me to.
Because if I do not, she will cry—wither maybe.
And my heart is too soft to hear such terrible sounds.
I am her mother after all. I did make her in my body.
     I must care for her, tend to the knots.

Speak
After Safia Elhillo

Jest.

Jambon.

French. English.

Spanish.

Farsi.

A word becomes a living room

anytime we speak the same tongue.

Family reunion. Give me French

and I will speak her like a sister.

Turkish and my aunt are old pals.

English naps on Mommon's lap like a family pet.

Each morning I hear the word   *bomb*

echo in a new accent.

Means threat.

Means safety.

Survival.

Kado.

A gift.

Language becomes   a bisquite

next to tea cups.

Jazeereh

an island

where Arabic and Farsi both break bread.

We ponder setareha together.

Ehsaas the way our mouths taste

the same sugar.

I am hungry for all our tongues.

But all I know are the keepers of our silence.

Joonam.

Azizeh del.

Eshgham.

I know how to say I love you

in a thousand different tongues.

Each word, its own country.

Each word, its own body standing

with its back against a border

praying with two palms pressed not to get shot.

Love is not a war zone

but most days it tastes like gunpowder.

Love is a home

you cannot go back to

but Khaleh tries to make a meal with it anyways.

Love is a living room

always telling you to enunciate.

Love emphasizes all the wrong syllables,

has broken English but dinner ready when you get home,

is not realizing my mother had an accent before someone pointed it out

because love never notices the things that do not affect it.

I find my name in the way my father says *hello*,

all Oklahoma and Iranian, how an ocean did not stop a man from

welcoming someone into his office.

My father builds shelters in a country where he has none.

Love is the flood that moved the car in Tehran.

Love is a boat full of men pulling a goat from the

water. It does not need a television for proof that it happened or exists.

Love breaks like earth in water. It lifts

all our dust. All the sediments of ourselves

we want to bury.

Welcome to Womanhood

After Trace Peterson

I confess I am no longer just a girl. No longer just
a woman or genitals or a face. Some days
my hoops are as big as my ego. My temper

sharper than a cat eye. I make
good tea and conversation from a man's
open mouth, lick honey

off my lover's ring finger. I've been
a sexless thing made of so many eyes
for too long. And now

I'm ready to be a dragon. I want to
drift out of this old box. Phoenix this dust
into a sunset. I want to be a wolf   a bitch   a huma

carrying me to old age.
This is girlhood remixed.
Buzzed heads and gapped teeth.

Chipped nails and my grandmother's perfume.
Gossip about boys with dull hair and unearned chins.
Girls with quick mouths and thumbs tucked in front pockets.

Womanhood, this home I rest my head in.
Kiss the hands of those I call *mother   sister   cousin.*
Offer the fruit that blooms in my chest.

This childhood bedroom where I learned to cut
out every magazine clipping from its place.
Pasted new freckles   fresh, uncut grass

found this wild chimera body,
a collage I knew how to fasten in myself.
This is womanhood. My girlhood

resurrected. Finger painted blue
brave in orange glitter. I run
through this meadow, moving joints

as a broad-backed boy   or girl   or ghost   or hippogriff.
This is still my firmer heart and porous skin.
In this home, I receive myself

in my tender body made of fuller calves   wide hips
and acne that stayed.
I claim myself.

I reclaim myself.
Fashion myself anew.
Welcome to womxnhood,

making vibrant soft
and soft in vibrant making.

Monterey Pine

Today I kiss the sun on both cheeks.
The saffron in Mommon's loobia polo
bows its head as it walks through the door.
Thank you, I say. *Merci*, megam.
I am grateful for the sharpness of the
carpet this morning. How blue and tactile
contentment seems. For each day, five
times, I clasp my hands and thank
the way my tea leaves spilled. Nod my head
in solidarity to the last day I saw his face.
How my ancestors tied me down
in those after hours. Let me bleed
for my own good. O the tears I
dropped at the ring of his name.
Now even on my crueler days, the pride
in Baba's lip rises like the moon.
Mommon beckons me to stay another night.
Take the couch. It is late.
Deerreh. Behmoon.
The clouds become a coat for an ice-tipped sky.
It is cold but our insides are
bundled and warm. I stopped
counting the minutes long ago.
I thank my lucky stars.

Notes

The line "orange juice with pulp" in "Epigraph From Anxiety on the Tarmac" is inspired by a line in Rudy Fransisco's "A Few Things I Believe" from his 2013 chapbook *Getting Stitches*.

The line "chewed me down to gristle" in "Date night" is inspired by a line in Zora Howard's "Before Bed" from its 2013 visual publication on The Strivers Row.

The form of "A List of Eleven..." is partially inspired by Chuck Wachtel's "A Paragraph Made Up of Seven Sentences" from Camille Paglia's 2006 critical anthology collection *Break, Blow, Burn*.

The phrase "bandaged apricots" in "Shame" is inspired by a phrase in Carrie Rudzinski's "The Prayer" from its 2012 visual publication on Speakeasynyc.

"Mohr" is partially inspired by the long-running American TV show *Supernatural*.

The phrase "a simple view/with a demanding hiking trail" in "Joy" is inspired by a line in Rudy Fransisco's "Complainers" from his 2017 debut collection *Helium*.

The line "I'm ready to be a dragon" in "Welcome to Womanhood" is inspired by Cecily Schuler's "My Gender Is" from its 2018 visual publication on SlamFind.

//

Immense gratitude to the editors and staff of the publications in which the following poems from this book were first published, sometimes in slightly different versions or earlier titles:

Porkbelly Press's *Love Me, Love My Belly* zine with "Soghatee";

Nat. Brut with "Khareji" and "Abody";

Two Idiots Peddling Poetry with their visual publications of "Ode to My Heart," "Learning to Pray," "Pussy Takes Herself Out," and "On Conflation";

Tinderbox Poetry Journal with "Ar-(Rahm)an";

BOAAT with "Family Tree";

Write About Now with their visual publication of "the heart has four cavities";

The Shallow Ends with "Things They Say—This is Not a Confessional.";

Juked with "The Man Holds the Door Open";

The Brown Orient with "Shame";

Moon Tide Press with their visual publication of "What is Sheila Sadr?";

Ghost City Press with "to the topless photos I took for an ex who asked";

Real Girls F.A.R.T. with their visual publications of "I am Letting Him Go Today" and "Joy."

Gratitude

The most profound gratitude to my mommon Zohreh and my baba Saeed; my siblings Shireen, Manijeh, Mohammad, and his wife Leyla; my grandma Azizam; and all my incredible extended family and ancestors for the energy, resilience, and love you have woven into my life. I love you more than you can ever imagine. I hope I've made you proud.

To the publishers, editors, designers, and staff at Not a Cult thank you for your spirit and dedication. Thank you Faye Orlove for your patience and sincerity, both beautifully reflected in this book's cover design. Thank you to Rhiannon McGavin for the joy, friendship, and heart you bring to everything you touch. Thank you especially to Daniel Lisi for believing in me and answering all my questions. Thank you for telling me to *never give them a story of submissiveness.*

I am extremely indebted to the poetry communities in Long Beach, Portland, Orange County, Los Angeles, and San Diego. Namely my deepest thank you to the staff, features, first-timers, and family—past and present—at The Definitive Soapbox. Thank you for giving me and so many others a home and a voice. Thank you also to the bundle of wonderfully tender and generous people who gather at Two Idiots Peddling Poetry, Slamlandia, the Portland Poetry Slam, Glassless Minds, and all their parking lots and living room floors. I can confidently say the world is a brighter place because you are beacons in it.

Massive thanks to California State University Long Beach's English-Creative Writing Department, Winter Tangerine's 2018 When the Moon Walks Workshop, The Speakeasy 2018 Summer Workshop Series, and the Spoken Literature Art Movement. Thank you for all the growth planted into my writing, community, and personhood.

To the beloved individuals who watched this book take its first steps (others are included in other sections)—Julia Gaskill, Keayva Mitchell, Paige Lewis, Bri Gowdy, Karla Cordero, torrin a. greathouse, Hanalena Fennel, my cousin Shawndeez Jadalizadeh, and the mighty Safia Elhillo—the power you all contain could supercharge a whole cityscape and further. You supernovas, I love you.

Thank you to all my mentors, guides, and teachers. Specifically, thank you Ms. Erin Topping Cusick, Ms. Laura Mayberry, Ms. Laura Holk, Professor David Hernandez, and Dr. Ilan Mitchell-Smith. Unending gratitude to my therapist Antionette. Thank you Edwin Bodney for your landscape of guidance from the very beginning. Thank you Yesika Salgado for the absolute gift you are to the world and thank you for always pushing me to take my first steps. Thank you Alyesha Wise-Hernandez and Matthew Cuban Hernandez for being my legitimate poetic parents. I genuinely don't know where I would be without your unending love. Thank you Antonio Cortez Appling for being my other poetry father. I cannot thank you and your entire family enough for the patience, warmth, and wisdom you've not only given to me but to our entire community. I love you all so much.

Thank you to all my friends. Thank you namely to Hannah Mishow, Jasmine "My Twin" Jafari, Abigail Pidazo, Jonathan "Humanoid" Werner, Alyssa Matuchniak, Marc "The Unmitigated Gall" J Cid, Kate Leddy, Devin Devine, Alice Giovanna, Elizabeth Chavez, Heather Parks, Chestina Craig, Victoria Gomez, Timothy "Big Brother" Cheung, Astríd, Derrick Engoy, Marilou Razo, Brian Sonia-Wallace, Charlie Oldham, and Kelly Grace Thomas. My goodness I love you.

To my circle, the loves of my life—Stephanie Carranza, Mikka Zanoria, and Sophia Warren—thank you for everything you do and are. Thank you for all the stories, the laughs, and the rescues. I wouldn't be here or who I am now without your radical authenticity, support, and love. There is a field of sunflowers in my heart for each of you. I love you so much.

And finally, thank you William. Thank you for everything. The endless lists of everything. You are my favorite. Stitched in the spaces between each line of this book is a secret love note for you. I love you.

Photo by Brian Gomez

About the Author

Sheila J Sadr is a first generation Iranian-American poet, performer, educator, and writer. She has had her work featured with the United Nations, TEDx, Segerstrom Center of the Arts, House of Blues, and many other gems. Sheila took first place at the 2018 UCI Jack Rabbit Poetry Slam and is a two time finalist for the Stories Award for Poetry, winning the second time around. She is currently pursuing her Master's in Clinical Psychology at Antioch University Los Angeles with a specialization in Trauma Studies and serves as the Talent Director for The Definitive Soapbox. This is her debut book.

sheilajsadr.com
Instagram: @ohohsheilaa